# The Character of Christian Ethics

The John Coffin Memorial Lecture
1977

# The Character of Christian Ethics

by
HELEN OPPENHEIMER

The John Coffin Memorial Lecture
delivered before the University of London
on 15 March 1977

UNIVERSITY OF LONDON
THE ATHLONE PRESS
1978

*Published by*
THE ATHLONE PRESS
UNIVERSITY OF LONDON
*at 4 Gower Street London* WCI

*Distributed by Tiptree Book Services Ltd*
*Tiptree Essex*

*U.S.A. and Canada*
*Humanities Press Inc*
*New Jersey*

© *University of London* 1978

ISBN 0 485 16211 3

ISSN 0449 0789

*Printed in Great Britain by*
*Western Printing Services Ltd*
*Bristol*

Christian ethics begins with the word 'repent'; what then are those of us doing who seek to commend it as thoroughly humanist? The posing of this question needs two explanations and an apology. First, no sharp distinction is intended between 'ethics' and 'morality'. Their meanings overlap, though 'ethics' has the more theoretical and 'morality' the more practical emphasis. Second, although the word 'humanist' is reserved by some to mean a Renaissance classical scholar and taken over by others to mean a contemporary sceptic, it still seems possible to use it to imply neither specialized meaning but simply to indicate someone who gives great moral importance to human beings.

Thirdly, an apology or anyway disclaimer seems called for. When Professor Peter Baelz gave his John Coffin Memorial lecture four years ago he was concerned lest in talking about Christian obedience he should 'be thought to have strayed from the paths of ethics and wandered into the field of theology'.[1] I ought to be the more concerned lest in asserting that Christian ethics begins with repentance I should be thought to have lapsed into plain Bible-thumping: to be presuming upon or ignoring the work of the New Testament critics, and to be preaching rather than analysing.

Let me reassure you that I am trying to embark upon a conceptual enquiry, not just an empirical one, still less a sermon; but where the field is Christian ethics the boundaries between these cannot be quite absolute. A conceptual enquiry has to have some data, some material to be enquired into, and there are two elementary difficulties about this: the difficulty about how much to assume, and the difficulty about how far to become involved. First, since we cannot all become Biblical experts before attempting to be any other sort of Christian scholar, something will have to be taken as given, either in simple faith or as an hypothesis. I am taking for granted the datum that the earliest account we have of Christ's ministry summarizes his initial teaching in a call to repent. Since the later tradition does not repudiate or minimize this aspect, I have to ask the moral not just historical question, Is there a deeper opposition than I am inclined to admit between Christian ethics and humanist ethics?

The second difficulty in making of this an academically respectable enquiry is already half explicit. The data of our faith, and particularly its ethics, however satisfactorily established, are not neutral matters of fact. To try to treat them as if they were would be to fall into the sin of Indifference identified by Edwin Muir: 'Nothing offending he is all offence, Can stare at beauty's bosom coldly and at Christ's crucifixion boldly.'² So maybe neither dogmatizing nor sermonizing can be avoided by the would-be Christian thinker. Having set up one's data one finds that the project of clarifying cannot be utterly separated from something like commending; and, worse still, that in this area all such activity will bring one under moral as well as intellectual judgement.

The problem I am trying to pose is that Christian ethics appears to have a tendency to fall apart into two necessary but inadequately related emphases; the reason why the problem seems to be worth posing is that one finds one's loyalties engaged on both sides of the division. The two emphases can be distinguished in various ways: for our present purposes they can be given the rough but convenient labels of 'religious' and 'humanist'. The 'religious' aspect of Christian ethics stresses obedience or disobedience to God's will, sin, and repentance; the 'humanist' aspect stresses love, goodness and fulfilment. The first tends to legalism, the second to antinomianism, but that controversy is not our immediate concern. Heteronomy, rule by another, versus autonomy, self-rule, is more directly in question; but the clearest contrast is between a high seriousness tending to gloom and a humane quest for happiness at the risk of being shallow. If one finds happiness the more attractive, one is the more bound to try to relate it satisfactorily to the other, more strenuous strand in Christian ethics, on the presumption that the strenuousness is at least as authentic as the good cheer. The call to repent and deny oneself, once acknowledged, seems to edge any kind of humanist aspiration out. To ask how far it has done so would be an historical enquiry: complicated, but plainly factual. To ask how far it needs to do so for Christianity to be ethically coherent is my present concern.

But it may well be asked, why be so anxious to keep the strand which I have called humanist within Christianity? Why not hang on as a Christian to the religious loyalty and let the humanism take care of itself? Is it not a temptation rather than a problem? Why not acquiesce in the sceptics' adoption of the name of 'humanist' and be content for Christians to be simply the people of God, turning their backs upon their unregenerate human wishes? One could not then lecture upon the character of Christian ethics; and perhaps that is a more genuine objection than might appear. For suppose that it is wrong to try to relate humanism to religion, and that a plain choice is called for: would such a 'plain choice' be a moral or an intellectual one, and could it be either without being the other? To give the matter full attention is not just a temptation confronting one's highest loyalty: it is entangled with one's highest loyalty.

It is of course a standard problem of faith, that Christian loyalty demands intellectual integrity and requires the thinking Christian to take on all comers, even those who threaten to undermine Christian loyalty.[3] But humanism is tangled with Christianity in a more specific way than this: there is an attack on Christian ethics as such which can be attractively answered by going a long way in a 'Christian humanist' direction. So, if one follows this line, a strong humanist strand is indeed woven into Christian ethics itself: it is not merely a cord pulling one out of true. It is some of the ramifications of this argument which I should like to explore. To see how the humanism gets in should give a better chance of seeing what right it has to be there.

The attack on Christian ethics is certainly an ethical attack. Its accusation is that Christianity, not just in practice but in principle, makes people less moral: juvenile at the best, self-seeking and obsequious not as an aberration but as a norm, because Christian morality is essentially heteronomous not autonomous. Christians have to obey God rather than form their own moral judgements.

The attack is by no means unanswerable. An answer has been finely outlined for example by Professor Baelz in his John Coffin lecture *Christian Obedience in a Permissive Context* in terms of 'a context of personal relationship, in which human freedom and fulfilment are to be realized in response to a transcendent reality which utters a word of claim and promise and reveals its gracious presence between man and man'.[4] It is because I am so completely convinced by this that it sets for me the further task of asking how far the ethic which results differs from a secular humanist ethic: in other words, to put it crudely, whether the battle has been won by proving too much. It is because I think the battle can be decisively won in this way that I have to ask: Can the Christian really have the best of both worlds? How is he *ethically* in a different position from the sceptical humanist? If one finds the ethic of personal response not only convincing but compelling, can one say, as one seems to want to say, both that acceptance of the Christian Gospel makes no difference in principle and that it makes all the difference? This is the position of Dorothy Sayers' advertiser whose slogan for margarine undermined any reason for buying butter.

To make this problem bite it is as well to go through some of the moves which lead into it. This can be done by imagining a square divided into four boxes, like a truth-table. The two top boxes represent theological ethics, the two lower ones secular ethics. There is a tendency to expect to find 'humanism' below rather than above, but let us leave that aside for the moment and make a different distinction. Cutting across the theological and the secular, let the two left-hand squares represent *naturalistic* ethics which get values from facts, and the two right-hand squares *non-naturalistic* ethics which emphasize the refusal to do so. Start then in the top left-hand corner with simple 'theological naturalism'. God *is* our Creator (fact) so we *ought* to obey Him (value). Hume's argument against getting an *ought* from an *is*[5] has, surely, permanently undermined this position. Right is right whether anyone is watching or not.[6] In reaction against any belief that ethics needs divine sanctions, there is a tendency to move digaonally across to secular non-naturalism: values must be our own choice: autonomy is a main point of any genuine morality.[7]

The Christian will be reluctant to settle in this secular position and will understandably want to remove himself back into some kind of theological ethic; but I do not believe he can do this by, as it were, moving straight up from secular non-naturalism into the box above, which I have labelled 'theological non-naturalism'. At first the move can sound promising. It goes like this. 'Of course value cannot come from bare fact, an ought from an is. Values must be chosen. But it is morally preposterous to think that we choose our own values. It is for God to do the choosing, in His sovereign majesty. Our good lies in His will.'

I have tried not to caricature this position, although it has led (from a humanist point of view) to some exceedingly unsatisfactory ethical beliefs, both Catholic and Protestant, about God's law and divine election. What is fundamentally wrong with it is that as an ethical position it collapses into the one with which we began. The two top compartments of the imaginary diagram cannot be kept apart, for it is not really possible to distinguish between taking God's will as an *is* from which we have to get our *ought*, and taking God's will as *His* choice by which *we* must abide. Both are liable to an objection older than Hume's, the ancient Euthyphro dilemma: do the gods command something because it is right, or is it right because the gods command it?[8] If God had commanded murder, would murder have been right? Is divorce wrong because and only because God forbids it? Theological ethics seems to be all of a piece and an easy target for logical and moral criticism. It is in this predicament that a Christian may discover (truly I believe) that the longest way round is the shortest way home, and that if he hopes to arrive at a properly theological ethic he must first go by way of the compartment untouched so far, secular naturalist ethics, which is willing to get its *ought* from the facts of human life, where values are not chosen but found.

In this compartment there is still room for choice. Human beings can and must choose *what to do*: in that sense they can choose good or evil. Eve could have refused the apple. More, they must often decide what *is* right, not just take orders: here lies their autonomy. They may do this creatively, not merely read it off from the facts. Perhaps Sartre's famous patriot may have an inspiration about what to do with his mother before he joins the Resistance movement.[9] But human beings cannot *decree* what *is to be* right. If I see a human being drowning, I may decide to plunge in, but I do not decide that he ought to be saved. I confer no value upon him: his plight claims my attention. We have to make our moral decisions according to what we find to be the case, however much we dislike saying that values can come from facts. We can say that a kind of Euthyphro dilemma is operating in this, non-theological, area of the diagram too. Is something supposed to be right because, not the gods this time, but autonomous moral agents, ordain that it shall be? Of course one feels a kind of reverence for autonomy, though maybe a partly superstitious reverence, which makes the naturalist horn of the dilemma hard to choose. Let me impale myself upon it.

What is good for people, let me say, putting the matter in a bluntly humanist but not necessarily sceptical way, is indeed what is *good* for people, that is, what is conducive to their true flourishing and not to their harm. *Ought* somehow comes from *is*, from what kind of beings we *are*, not from what we, the gods, or anyone else, decide to think.[10]

It would be only too easy to beg the question here. 'True flourishing' is a very slippery concept when it is human beings we are dealing with. As Miss Anscombe has pointed out, it is all very well to talk about the flourishing of something simple like a plant; that is 'not at all fishy';[11] but who is to say what is to *count* as the flourishing of a human being? Sooner or later it looks as if somebody will have to *decide* and we shall be back with non-naturalism.

Yet I think the main point the naturalist wants to make survives and can be put like this. To the non-naturalist, only choice can so to speak get morality moving. Facts are inert: we assemble all the facts and *then*, as a separate exercise, we evaluate. But this is to define fact as neutral, as outside morality, and maybe what the naturalist is doing is simply cast doubt on this definition and urge us to look more closely at the interplay between fact and value. He would insist that to suppose that the world consists of bare value-free facts on which 'evaluations' somehow confer goodness is an illusion or at best an abstraction.

For example, torture is wrong because human beings dislike being hurt, not just because we decide to deplore it. To make all the value come from choosing can actually belittle choice by making it, precisely, arbitrary: assimilating it almost to tossing a coin. Values must be more adequately related than this to facts. What the sceptic says of God's will turns out to apply to any will: a sovereignty which is total is ethically meaningless. If moral choice is to be significant it must have something factual to go on.

Everybody in this argument is opposed to an arbitrary morality. The naturalist is against the arbitrariness of making values depend on choice; but the non-naturalist for his part remains reluctant to tie values to fact because that seems to put moral principles at the mercy of what just happens to be. Perhaps he can be reassured by a closer look at the idea of 'just happening to be'. Torture is wrong because we hate to be hurt, but it does not just happen to be wrong because we do not just happen to hate to be hurt. Morality changes if the facts change, but some sorts of facts are, as it were, conceptually recalcitrant to change. Not all human beings can, logically, be masochists or the word would lose its meaning. If human beings generally had liked pain, we may be tempted to say that it would have been our duty to inflict it; but then we should not have called it 'pain' or 'inflict'. The argument has fallen into nonsense here because 'pain' is not a neutral term. Not to be liked is part of its meaning. But to find a substitute that is neutral enough to yield an alternative morality is surprisingly hard. 'If human beings had liked being stabbed . . .' One can tell a story about this, but it will have to be rather a complex story, turning on what they like it for. If such liking is neither perverse nor part of a wider aim it is hard to render it coherent in terms of the concept of a personal being. One can say piquant things as long as one does not attempt to develop them. 'Fate urged the sheers, and cut the Sylph in twain, (But Airy Substance soon unites again).'[12] To enquire into the biology of this would be swiftly to become embroiled in an essentially philo-sophical enquiry about what one could mean by a body which was not vulnerable to ordinary harm: to whom injury did not matter.

The moral man can therefore be assured that moral principles are safe even on a naturalist view because there could not be a moral world much different from this. A good look at the facts is bound to yield a recognizable morality. It does not just 'happen' to be true that personal beings dislike pain, that they have purposes, that they communicate with one another, that they want to survive; and therefore that they are damaged by the kinds of actions that they are damaged by and that we hold to be wrong: violence, lies, the withholding of goodwill.[13] It does not seem too much to say that elementary ideas of justice and even of love are built in to the very concept of a person, a moral being. 'Built-in value' seems a more useful notion than 'bare fact'. So if facts are not bare we can go on getting our values from them; a frankly humanist morality of what is good for us is not unprincipled but is an entirely legitimate basis for enquiring logically into the character of ethics.

All this may seem miles away from Christian ethics, but on the contrary it is my contention that here, in the area where values come from facts and good from flourishing, the Christian is not in such a strange country as he would be in the area where values come from choices. From this side of the diagram there are two possible routes back into a theological ethic; whereas from the ethics of choice I can see only the route that leads into the Euthyphro dilemma. The ways I am proposing head towards a kind of 'theological naturalism', that is, towards the top left-hand square where we began; but as they now find quite different scenery there it is possible that our diagram has become three dimensional and the paths through secular ethics and back sloping rather than flat.

To take the simpler of the two routes we seize on to the notion of flourishing and take it into theological territory. The Christian has learnt from the humanist that to flourish is good for us in a properly ethical sense. Now is the time for him to ask about the *true* flourishing of a human being. He may insist that any sceptical humanism takes too short-term a view of what it is to flourish. It is eternal life that counts, the ultimate flourishing which makes all merely human well-being trivial by comparison. So we slip back into theology. By this easy path there is hardly a frontier between the two naturalist areas of the diagram. Between the theological and the non-theological here there is no ethical difference, only a difference of fact: are we God's creatures, whose true flourishing is to live in His heaven? If so, then morality does come from God, but from *the way he has created the world*, not from His arbitrary fiat. The fact, if fact it be, that God *is* our creator is not after all irrelevant to what we *ought* to do, but is just what we need to fill in the concept of human nature so that it can give us enough to go on morally. So we can fall back on theology, not on choice, when the non-naturalist goes on insisting that the world cannot yield a morality.

But the revolt which is now inevitable is a religious revolt, not a philosophical one, against the humanist presuppositions of this whole argument. Far from being the centre of our ethics, God has become a kind of prop for human concerns. This is not to say that human concerns must be selfish concerns. Humanism need not be egoism, and human flourishing need not be primarily one's own flourishing. Nor need the emphasis be materialistic: the most celebrated people who believed in happiness, the Epicureans, were ascetics not libertines. But the more 'spiritual' and heavenly the idea of flourishing is made, the less it looks like the complete ethical answer. How dare a Christian suppose that there is nothing more ethically important than happiness, however loftily conceived? Even if duty is not to be set above happiness, the holiness of God can surely not be measured by such a puny yardstick. So the easier route is open to the criticism that it has seemed easy because it has not led into the heart of Christian ethics at all.

The other route back from secular to theological naturalism may be harder but looks more promising, because instead of moving straight from earthly flourishing to Christian morality it picks up and relates to theology the more difficult idea of 'built-in value'. Rather than being so much concerned with what does us good, its way of getting morality from facts is to think in terms of *claims* upon us. It will reiterate that a bare, neutral fact is an abstraction, a limiting concept, so that to keep fact and value apart is apt to be a hopeless exercise. Morality is not a matter of putting in the values but of *responding* to the values we find built in to the way things are. To be capable of making this kind of moral response is what makes us human, so we can still call ourselves humanist; but the way is wide open to make our humanism theological. Claims in principle may be infinite, and the highest claim we can think of is the love of God, if He exists.

I seem to have made God's love hypothetical. What I have not made it is vague. The theology into which this route leads is specifically, it may be thought narrowly, Christian, not just theist. If the love of God is to elicit response in this kind of way, as a claim built in to a fact, it must be quite crudely factual not inaccessibly metaphysical. What I am talking about here is indeed the Cross, which Christians believe exhibits the limitless love of God in definite human terms. To affirm this is more than to put love at the centre of morality and then to call Jesus divine because he showed this love. It is to describe Christianity as the religion for which values cost God something, in other words to commit oneself to a high Christology with all the strenuous metaphysical wrestling which that must involve. The obligation to undertake such wrestling can be seen as part of the moral response one must make to the Christian claim. The present point is that *if* facts can be seen as having values built into them and so as constituting claims, and *if* it is a fact that 'God was in Christ reconciling the world to himself', *then* Christians can make this fact ethically central, as both calling forth their highest response and encouraging them to build all their responses into one system. They may accept the label of 'theological naturalism' without succumbing to Hume's strictures, for they find their *ought* in an *is*, but not in a neutral *is*. As for the Euthyphro dilemma, they are as well placed as anyone else for facing it. God commands what *is* right; but the heart of value is what God Himself *is*.

To me, this ethic is wholly convincing. I could say indeed that it is 'what I believe'. It can be spelt out in detail in terms of various favourite key words: response, relationship, love, and particularly *personality*. God is, as it were, Top Person, and Christian ethics on this view is not a special kind of morality but is more, much more, of the morality of being a person. It can be clarified, characterized, commended as a transcendent ethic, an ethic of grace, picking up everything that human beings take as valuable and finding it all owing to, and vindicated by, God's creative love. To explore all this is not something different from exploring Christianity itself.

But I cannot offer it as the answer to the problem with which I began; on the contrary, it sets the problem with which I began, by inserting this large 'humanist' wedge into Christian ethics. If morality is a matter of finding and responding to value, and especially the value of persons, it looks as if in the last resort we judge God, however, much we claim to find ourselves wanting. We have our own system of values and make Him its coping stone, and we have to ask whether a Christian ethic can tolerate, still less be proud of, such an order of procedure. Must humanism, however it may make itself at home, be a cuckoo in the Christian nest?

It is tempting to brush aside the criticism as superficial, and simply reassert that an ethic of personal relationship, exemplified in a humble and joyful response to God's love as shown on the Cross, is a long way from the negative or rebellious humanism of the sceptic. Indeed this is what one hopes eventually to have the right to say. All that follows is an attempt at consolidation not at starting all over again, but the consolidation needs to be fairly radical. For it is no small matter that if one brings this carefully set-up theological naturalism to a re-reading of, say, St Mark's Gospel or St Paul's Epistles, one finds oneself either breathing or suffocating in what I can only call a much more 'religious' ethical atmosphere. The standard way of saying this is that Christian ethics are *theocentric*, but the party feelings this could arouse would be a distraction. It seems preferable to fall flop into the truism that Christian ethics are, after all, religious ethics. They seem to start, not at the threshold of the ethical route we have been following, but in a place where it is over-whelmingly assumed that the initiative is God's and that human beings have nothing of their own to offer: a place where Karl Barth is more at home, and does more justice to humanity, than our humanist contemporaries.[14]

Christian ethics are not comfortably portrayed as the crown of a system but a turning again into something new. 'Response' is by no means an unsuitable word, but it is cast for a less splendid role than theological naturalism would give it. To give God the prize as Chief Value seems not to reckon with the fundamental Christian con-viction that the Gospel somehow makes all the difference, that it is ethically life-giving and not merely life-enhancing. The text St Augustine was wont to quote, 'What hast thou that thou hast not received?'[15] can come as an intellectual rebuke: not that ethical analysis is wrong, but that one had better analyse what Christianity is really about. If 'repent and believe the Gospel' is an embarrass-ment, one is on the wrong lines.

At this juncture one can find philosophical comfort, as so often, in the commonplace wisdom that 'things have to be worse before they are better'. Christian humanism may be as suspect to humanists as it is to Christians. It is not much use simply to nominate the system of values one happens to find inspiring as what everyone must really mean by morality. Disconcerting as it may be, it is reasonable for both sides to complain at such a proceeding: the Christian, that divine values are being accommodated to the world; the humanist, that he is being colonized into a foreign kingdom; and both, that would-be Christian humanism is naive. It is unrealistic for the Christian to expect the sceptical humanist to sit down sadly saying 'I respond to all your values but alas there is no God to vin-dicate them'. He is much more likely to set out and find values of his own, some of which the Christian will deplore. So the 'religious' and the 'humanist' strands pull apart. They have not been properly woven together, only tangled.

Yet the Christian cannot be content merely to disentangle them. He still needs to relate them to each other, to say both that Chris-tianity does make all the difference and that it does not. He is still the advertiser trying to sell both butter and margarine. The point of all the argument so far has been to exhibit this as a real problem, not something which can be solved for the Christian by simply scrapping his humanist tendencies. He is committed, to some extent, to the margarine. To recommend a naturalist ethic of built-in values to which one responds as a human being is to allow that in some sense Christianity does not make all the difference.

At one level this need not be a very alarming admission. It is only to accept, what is surely evident, that some at least of one's fellow human beings have a real, objective morality. To grant them this a Christian may be allowed a little colonizing and a little accommodation. He must colonize to the extent of being ready to welcome his sceptical contemporaries as fellow citizens of a moral world. He must accommodate in not claiming that morality consists simply in obedience to God's commands. But this particular Christian will not especially want obedience as a keyword, for his concern is to interpret ethics, and Christian ethics in particular, in terms of a loving response.

The trouble is that if the Christian concedes so much he will have to concede more. This line of thought is losing any right to give Christianity any ethical advantage. If one has brought the humanist along so far one has no right to abandon him just here, where ethics begins to get humanly interesting. To insist on his company to help one discover that objective values can be built into facts makes it very difficult suddenly to bar him from the higher reaches of morality where the values turn out to be personal. Just because one has planned all along to make 'loving response' one's keyword, one has not thereby acquired proprietary rights in it. If morality as such is not a Christian monopoly, then neither is love. The idea of response to built-in value keeps leading to what Christians and unbelievers have in common. The capacity to love has to do with what human beings as such are, whether they are Christians or not. Far from being able to distinguish Christian and unbeliever, loving response may be what remains when faith and hope are gone. It is not just that love will abide when faith and hope have been swallowed up in fulfilment, but that it is what we should have to cling to if they perished. If there were no built-in values in the universe we should be left saying with Matthew Arnold 'Ah love, let us be true to one another!'[16] But then it is hard to say that Christianity adds anything to our ethic, only to our hopes. Christian ethics seems to be shouldered out. Butter is only expensive margarine.

There is an answer to this which I have approached before and which can now be fairly grasped. It is to link basic Christian morality to creation, rather than essentially to redemption. Creation came in before when we were facing the objection that God's commands must be arbitrary not ethical.[17] The provisional reply emerged that morality arises from the way God has created the world, not from his blank fiat. Now this can be taken up and linked with the morality of response. We can respond because we were made so. Christian ethics is no more shouldered out because there was love before the Christian gospel than Christian theology is shouldered out because there was religion before the Christian gospel. Each finds a basis in what God has put there first.

What God has 'put there' morally is a world of human beings who are capable of love. A Christian therefore has the right to be as humanist as God the Creator. 'What a piece of work is a man! How noble in reason! How infinite in faculty! ... the beauty of the world! The paragon of animals!' Even if he goes on to say 'And yet, to me what is this quintessence of dust?' or, more piously, to talk about the Fall and the need for reconciliation, he can still locate the capacity for response in human beings as such, not only in Christians. This capacity is the foothold for redemption, not the result of redemption. So ethics can be rooted, as the 'naturalist' wants to say, in human nature; and if human nature is rooted in God the 'no difference/ all the difference' difficulty is not insoluble. The grace of God is for a Christian the bedrock of the universe. It is something we can as it were dig down to. The sceptical humanist has not yet dug deep enough but he is digging in the same soil as the believer.

To make a theology of creation fundamental to ethics but as it were buried makes it possible for the Christian moralist to exercise a greater patience in locating God's presence: it is basic enough that it can be allowed to be as unobtrusive, or as noticeable, as we may find it to be. Either way, it is not peripheral. One can proceed as a philosopher or moralist and let one's Christianity underlie the whole argument without having to be made explicit at every turn on pain of disloyalty. So, if we can contentedly give up the attempt to *distinguish* Christian ethics at once from secular ethics, we can try with a better hope to *characterize* the ethic we hold as Christians, and even eventually to see its real distinctiveness, and all this still in terms of response.

Response is somehow both normal and special. So far we have stressed its normality: it has to do with what human beings are. But one cannot talk long about the human capacity to respond to built-in value without some attention to what I have called the higher reaches of morality where the values turn out to be personal. The notion of response, brought in to stress that morality is a human affair, leads quickly into complications. One finds oneself talking, still humanly, about *Two Moralities*, a lower level of basic requirements and a higher level where response becomes in some sense transcendent. When a Christian has grasped that he has no monopoly even of the transcendent level, but does not need to have, he is in a better position to sort out some of the complexities of this way of talking and see what his particular contribution to it is after all. The Christian Gospel clearly has something to do with transcendence. The question still is to see what. In a way, the 'no difference/all the difference' problem simply moves on; but it should with a little care become more manageable.

The main reason for care is that there are a number of overlapping but different ways of talking about Two Moralities, not all of which have much to do with response. In separating levels of morality people have had a number of distinctions in mind, mostly variations on the theme of the legal and the personal. They include the contrasts between the compulsory and the optional; precepts and counsels; legalism and love; crime and sin; nature and grace; law and gospel; social morality and individual ideal; letter and spirit; demand and inspiration; outward and inward; rule and creation. The notion of response needs to be tracked through this thicket, by tracing the legal/personal theme through these contrasts.

The simplest distinction, which is apt to bedevil all the others, is the distinction between the *compulsory and the optional*. The hunt is on for a transcendent ethic when this is seen to be inadequate. Some things can be demanded of us; others can be asked; but some asking is practically demanding, at least for some people. It is hopeless to try to force people into the world of grace, whether with spiritual or with physical sanctions, but how dare we leave them outside? To say 'You must go beyond duty' is unreasonable, but to say 'You may; you need not' is morally inadequate. Traditional Christian moralists have long debated this problem in the terminology of *precepts and counsels*;[18] it was drawn to the attention of philosophers in 1958 in an article by Mr Urmson called 'Saints and Heroes'.[19]

The easiest answer, which is not an answer at all, is to let the compulsory and the optional share out morality between them. This can be done quite legalistically in a morality of Two Standards, of basic demands for the many and works of supererogation for the few. Nowadays, the compulsory is out of fashion and of the two the optional is more likely to prevail. This is revealed by the use of the word 'ideal' to characterize the higher morality of *love* in contrast with *legalism*. It is not much use though to get rid of the legalistic word 'supererogation' unless the idea can also be eliminated; and when one is told, for instance, 'Christ did not legislate: he laid ideals before us' it is a short step to conclude tacitly that the ideals need hardly ever become actual, that the highest flights are only for the few. Here, among Protestant Christians who repudiate the old Two Standards ethic of monasticism, is the makings of a new Two Standards ethic which offers no prizes for reaching the higher level, but which is just as unable to relate them.

From this the ethic of personal response offers release. What needs to be understood is that the higher morality is not of the same kind as the lower morality, and must somehow leave *both* the compulsory and the optional behind on the lower level. The Christian at this stage can help the argument best by not hindering. He may be tempted here to go off on a line of his own. He may like the look of the distinction between *crime and sin*, and be led by it to miss the point. This distinction is generally used to distinguish the demanding the law of the land does from other kinds of claims. It is a convenient device for the liberal-minded lawyer to stop penalizing some offences without denying that they do indeed offend. But the whole concept of offence remains in the world of the compulsory. If a theologian seizes on to the word 'sin' and defines it as offence against the law of *God* he will only short-circuit the discussion. It is the optional this time which is abolished, not transcended. God's commands have a stringency which is too much for us.

The theologian may think that he has a way through by going deeper into theology, by contrasting *nature and grace*. Of course we cannot ourselves cope with God's commands. It is for God, not man, to do the transcending. Talk about human capacity for response is all very well, but the proper response to God's goodness is only possible when nature is crowned by grace or, in more Protestant style, *law* is swallowed up in *gospel*. The Christian preacher certainly has a message for the poor sinner who is stuck on the compulsory side of the divide, a message of two moralities indeed, in which God and God alone can move us up to the higher level. The trouble is that though this may be theology, it is not ethics. The sinner who cannot measure up to God's demands is to be snatched up to the higher level, according to his churchmanship, either by an application of divine grace seen as something verging on the magical, or by being accounted righteous in the midst of his sins.

The difficulty comes from making expressly Christian contrasts too quickly. The religiously neutral distinction between the legal and the personal deserves more patience than this from the Christian believer. The theological concept of grace is not to be approached head-on like this. The grace of God can be exhibited as a truly ethical term if it is approached by a more roundabout route. We must look where grace is to be found in human life, not just at the gap we want it to fill. The question to ask is Oman's question, 'What is a moral personality, and how is it succoured?'[20] The point of grace, human or divine, is that it enables by eliciting response: response is still both special and normal.

What an ethic of response does is transcend the whole compulsory/optional division by making it irrelevant, by opening up a world where one no longer wants to ask the deadly question, 'Do I have to?' It is this moral capacity for going beyond basic morality that makes human life worth living, whether we put the emphasis on its fragility and finiteness and need for the supernatural grace of God, or on the splendours that human beings can sometimes be seen to achieve. Once we have arrived at an 'ethic of response' it is open to us to Christianize it. If we are Christians, it cannot be open to us not to.

This potentially theological way of talking need not nowadays be an embarassment to a philosopher. There has been, within the last twenty years, a considerable enrichment of philosophical ethics. Lord Lindsay's strictures in *The Two Moralities* on academic philosophy as standing 'mainly remote and aloof'[21] from the morality which makes 'the challenge to perfection'[22] is now undeserved. Mrs Warnock protested vigorously in 1960 about 'the increasing triviality of the subject'[23] and especially the unimportance of the examples philosophers had favoured. Mr Urmson's reminder that there is heroism and sanctity as well as decent behaviour has been heard.[24] The moralist and the moral philosopher need no longer live in different worlds, and embarrass each other if they ever hold converse. Sometimes they can be the same person. The point that ethics are about what concerns us deeply has been well taken, and philosophers such as Professor Strawson are now concerned to indicate the richness of ethics, both in the variegated images of human life which it creates, and in the complex inter-relations between aspects of *social* and *individual* morality.[25]

It must seem ungrateful to doubt that these developments do justice to the transcendent aspects of morality in which Christians are interested. But the secular philosopher is no more immune than the Christian theologian from slipping back into, or never quite rising above, the compulsory/optional dichotomy. The notion of an effectively optional higher realm of ethics is having a lively existence in eminent non-theological circles. Again it is the word 'ideal' which indicates that the optional is being allowed to win.

I should hardly like to describe Professor Strawson's important article, 'Social Morality and Individual Ideal' as a Trojan horse; but it is possible that its very sensitivity could be confusing to Christian moralists, because the position it espouses is so like and yet not quite like what I have been calling an ethic of response. Professor Strawson's article is a subtle and authoritative discussion of a 'two moralities' theme. I must presume to register a kind of dissatisfaction with it, just because the individual ideals cannot escape from being optional ideals. He does indeed give an important place to response. We get beyond our accepted social morality and warm to images of assorted forms of life. But the response evoked is not of the transcendent sort I have been trying to indicate, but is rather 'a response of the liveliest sympathy from those whose own patterns of life are as remote as possible from conformity to the image expressed'.[26] The imagination may be captivated,[27] but not, in the old sense, the heart. The conflicting images expressly remain conflicting and even incompatible.[28]

Unless one is a fanatic, it may seem greedy to ask for more than this. A Christian moralist may be so grateful to be appreciated and to be given such agreeable cause to appreciate the values of others, that he is content to go very little further. He cannot of course concur that the competing ideals may at last be irreconcilable. His belief in God assures him that though there may be many valid vocations there are not in the end incompatible truths. Nor will he think 'appreciation' goes far enough: he must respond, and respond not only with his sympathy but with his life; but he will find that Professor Strawson can ungrudgingly allow him this. Christian morality can find its place, not merely tolerated but admired, among the ethical ideals. The price is that an ideal is what it remains, optional rather than compulsory, or compulsory only for the few. The Two Moralities are still Two Standards.

The trouble is that the meaning of 'transcendence' is gently set aside, not explored. The Christian may have his 'single intense vision',[29] which certainly *goes beyond* the claims of ordinary social morality; but the use of the word 'ideal' inhibits analysis of what such 'going beyond' could mean. The higher level of morality remains optional, though maybe magnificently so, or tyrannical.

It would be unreasonable to expect a liberal philosopher to do the committed moralist's work for him and work out how the higher level of morality can be transcendent. But it would be a pity if the distinction between social and individual morality, when made as authoritatively and subtly as this, were allowed to obscure this problem and encourage us to be satisfied with an ethic in which whatever is not compulsory is optional. Rather we want to shed the word 'ideal' and talk of two moralities in terms of *letter and spirit*. The higher level is where people are able to reap the harvest of the spirit, to do more than could be required of them; and the small 's' for 'spirit' is a convenient ambiguity still.

What we have arrived at is still not a simple contrast of levels. The concept of spirit as opposed to letter can distinguish two moralities in answer to several different anxieties. If it is the terrible stringency of the *demands* of law that strikes us, we can find ourselves liberated by the idea that personal response is not another and stricter requirement but is a matter of *inspiration*. If our concern is that obeying the letter of the law is a matter of merely *external* conformity, we can stress that the personal morality of grace is *inward*, is 'written on the heart'. If it is the mechanical aspect of law that dissatisfies us, the concept of *creative* inspiration belongs here too[30] in contrast with a morality of *rules*. Some people will especially want to stress that this sort of morality goes beyond 'the letter' as laid down in set rules;

that it is something made, an 'artifice';[31] that it brings something new, imaginative and maybe unpredictable into being, that 'out of three sounds' it can 'frame, not a fourth sound, but a star'.[32]

But this cannot be the whole story. In propounding Christian ethics as not distinctively but characteristically an ethic of response I have not got rid of the suspicion that the humanist tendencies, which I neither can or want to expunge, leave out something central. There remains a theoretical not only a practical inadequacy about the ethic of human response when it is measured against the basic demand to *turn again* and believe the Gospel.

It is easy enough to brush aside as hopelessly exaggerated the Protestant insistence that human morality is not only weak but corrupt, that 'it is precisely morality which *is* evil',[33] that man-centredness is rootedly opposed to God-centredness. Professor Hepburn has taken a fairly short way with these ideas in *Christianity and Paradox,* [34] and of course one feels that any healthy-minded thinker, Christian or not, must be on his side; and yet the last word has not been said. To think this is not a matter of terrible sternness or intractable gloom, still less of wallowing in the idea of sinfulness; these are indeed aberrations. What one finds rather if one dips into Karl Barth, or still more if one returns to the Gospels and Epistles to which he points, is a refreshing light-heartedness precisely from having shed the anxieties of humanism.

The ethic of human response does indeed transcend the legal ethic of rights and duties; and it does this best, and a Christian will add most characteristically, when what it responds to is the glory of God. This ethic is not, emphatically not, to be invalidated; but is it nonsense to say that it may need to be transcended in its turn? For to stop with human response is still to stake a claim, a claim which ought at last to be left behind, as response leaves behind but does not invalidate law.

The historic slogan for this development is *justification by faith,* which of course can have many meanings, some of them notoriously much less satisfactory than the ethic of response I have been trying, on this side idolatry, to commend. What at its best justification by faith can indicate is the active dependence of all goodness upon God:[35] the positive, not the negative abandonment of human works and human worth in the face of the holiness of God. It is not that human beings are unworthy any more than law is unethical, but that their own worthiness is not something to be lingered upon when they could be celebrating the glory of God. Belief in God no more extinguishes human goodness than sunshine blows out a candle. Human goodness is as real as we could wish, but wholly derivative. To quote St Augustine again, 'When God crowns our merits, he crowns nothing but his own gifts.'[36]

It is when thoughts about human worthiness, or unworthiness, distract attention from God's glory that one wants to say that good works have the nature of sin and that human morality is actually evil. It can come to look like a huge apparatus for ignoring the one thing needful. The attempt to justify oneself can be to turn one's back on the absolute for the sake of the relative. The relentless insistence that one is not in the wrong, that one has acted justly, can become a sickly and damaging form of corruption, more deceptive than the straightforward brutal sins for which human beings blame each other. The saints are apt to see this high-minded self-love as *the* real sin. It is the last sin to keep a hold; and it is far from seeming the least for those who are in a position to say, 'Late have I loved thee, beauty so ancient and so new.'[37]

All this could be said, with care, in the language of response, but it has an emphasis which the language of response even in its Christian form could miss and which the language of pure humanism must miss by definition. What it is asserting is that in an important ethical sense being right is no good when confronted with holiness. Holiness destroys ethics, not by invalidating it but by going beyond it, and what Christianity confronts us with is holiness. So the response which it elicits is essentially a turning again, not a continuing in the same moral line even at a new level.

What I am suggesting is a kind of three-tier ethic: naturalist, because at each level claim is built in to fact. I do not want to exclude the secular humanist from any, though he may exclude himself from the third. The first two levels are, very roughly, the level of objective demand where the compulsory and the optional belong, and the level of transcendent response. As a Christian sees it, both these levels belong to creation, not only to redemption, and are therefore still there for someone who does not believe in God as much as creation is still there. How far they are impoverished for the unbeliever is a matter of emphasis.

What I want to emphasize now is that Christian humanism sees the creation not as rotten, but as *vulnerable*. All human ethics, including the ethics of response, is a good but fragile thing. It is appropriate to say, with any amount of gratitude 'How far that little candle throws his beams'; to be concerned for its flickering; or to see it fade in the sun. There is no need to be dissatisfied with it: unless it fails. What Christianity propounds is an ethic which can survive failure: which can 'make all the difference' by way not of improvement but of resurrection. To give up every claim is not to be lost but to receive all blessings, and to die is not destruction but the prelude to being reborn. The giving up must not be self-conscious, precisely not, any more than the death is to be suicidal. They are to happen when they are required of us. So we could still characterize this aspect of Christian ethics under the heading of an ethic of response, so long as the point of response is its spontaneity not its virtue. But I should like, not just for the sake of tidiness, to find another word for this 'level' of Christian ethics, to take up and add to the words characterizing the previous levels. The word 'faith' suggests itself, as I have talked about 'justification by faith'; but it could have too subjective a flavour. It is too near in meaning to 'response'; and it could turn back on itself. As F. D. Maurice put it, one can 'believe justification by faith, instead of believing in Christ the Justifier'.[38] The word 'grace' strongly suggests itself, and is indeed what I mean; but I should like to look for another word which has been less stiffened by theological controversies.

May I suggest that Christian ethics at its most characteristic is, first, an ethic of objective demand; and second, an ethic of response; but that, thirdly, it is still more an ethic of *mercy*. I am still not wanting to rule out the unbeliever, for of course there is a human mercy too; but it is the mercy *of God* which is really in question, and that almost in the sense of his immanence.[39] Human goodness is not just human response, not even just response to what God is and has done, but has to do with God's goodness acting *in* us.[40] Mercy is not just a graciousness which is ready to pick up the pieces when something has gone wrong. It is the oil in the works, not just the oil in the wounds.[41] Indeed it is more than that: it is the substance of God's condescension. It is the form God's sovereign love takes when it enters into creation to enable it to be what God made it for. This is what faith believes in, and what makes response possible. It undermines humanism and all human pretensions and then sets up humanism again on a new foundation. It is because of God's mercy that glory in human beings, rightly understood, is included in glory in God.

# NOTES

1. Peter Baelz, *Christian Obedience in a Permissive Context*, The John Coffin Memorial Lecture 1973, p. 5.
2. Edwin Muir, *Collected Poems* (1960), p. 50.
3. Cf. Hugo Meynell, 'The Euthyphro Dilemma', *Proceedings of the Aristotelian Society*, Supplementary Volume XLVI (1972), p. 229.
4. Peter Baelz, op. cit., p. 25.
5. Hume, *A Treatise of Human Nature*, III, 1, i.
6. Cf. R. Hepburn, *Christianity and Paradox*, p. 135.
7. Cf. R. Hare, *Freedom and Reason*, pp. 1–2.
8. Cf. A.C.C.M., *Teaching Christian Ethics*, pp. 71–3.
9. J-P. Sartre, *Existentialism and Humanism*, pp. 35–6.
10. I have discussed this further in *The Character of Christian Morality* (Second Edition) Chapter IX, and in 'Ought and Is' printed in *Duty and Discernment*, ed. G. R. Dunstan.
11. 'Modern Moral Philosophy', *Philosophy* (1958), p. 7.
12. Pope, *The Rape of the Lock*, III, 151–2.
13. Cf. H. Hart, *The Concept of Law*, p. 176.
14. Cf. Barth, *The Humanity of God*.
15. 1 Cor. 4: 7, e.g. Sermon 43.
16. 'Dover Beach.'
17. See above, p. 12.
18. Cf. K. Kirk, *The Vision of God*, pp. 240–57.
19. Printed in *Essays in Moral Philosophy*, ed. A. I. Melden.
20. Oman, *Grace and Personality*, p. 45.
21. Lindsay, *The Two Moralities*, p. 8.
22. Ibid., p. 9 and e.g. p. 46.
23. M. Warnock, *Ethics since 1900*, p. 202.
24. See above, note 19.
25. P. F. Strawson, 'Social Morality and Individual Ideal', *Philosophy* (1961), printed in *Freedom and Resentment*, cf. pp. 28ff, p. 43.
26. Ibid., p. 27.
27. Ibid., p. 26.
28. Ibid., p. 44.
29. Ibid.
30. I have discussed this aspect in 'Moral choice and divine authority' printed in *Christian Ethics and Contemporary Philosophy*, ed. I. T. Ramsey.
31. Cf. G. R. Dunstan, *The Artifice of Ethics*.
32. Browning, 'Abt Vogler'.

33. Brunner, *The Divine Imperative*, p. 71; cf. Bultmann, *Essays*, e.g. p. 40.

34. pp. 142–4.

35. Cf. Vincent Taylor, e.g. *Forgiveness and Reconciliation*, chapter II; Austin Farrer, *Saving Belief*, pp. 113–14; *Said or Sung*, p. 74; Keith Ward, *Ethics and Christianity*, pp. 245, 255.

36. Ep. 194 19. See J. Burnaby, *Amor Dei*, p. 238.

37. *Confessions*, X, 27.

38. F. D. Maurice, *Theological Essays*, p. 153.

39. A theme I have discussed in *Incarnation and Immanence*.

40. Cf. Burnaby, *Amor Dei*, p. 277; Farrer, *Interpretation and Relief*, pp. 95–100.

41. Cf. A. Bloom, *Living Prayer*, pp. 86–7.